'You r[...]
Odyss[...], man
of twists and
turns . . .'

HOMER
Date and location of birth and death unknown

HOMER IN PENGUIN CLASSICS
The Homeric Hymns
The Iliad
The Odyssey

HOMER

Circe and the Cyclops

Translated by
Robert Fagles

PENGUIN BOOKS

PENGUIN CLASSICS

UK | USA | Canada | Ireland | Australia
India | New Zealand | South Africa

Penguin Books is part of the Penguin Random House group of companies
whose addresses can be found at global.penguinrandomhouse.com.

Penguin
Random House
UK

This selection published in Penguin Classics 2015
004

Set in 9.5/13 pt Baskerville 10 Pro
Typeset by Jouve (UK), Milton Keynes
Printed in Great Britain by Clays Ltd, St Ives plc

A CIP catalogue record for this book is available from the British Library

ISBN: 978-0-141-39861-7

www.greenpenguin.co.uk

MIX
Paper from
responsible sources
FSC® C018179

Penguin Random House is committed to a
sustainable future for our business, our readers
and our planet. This book is made from Forest
Stewardship Council® certified paper.

Contents

In the One-Eyed Giant's Cave

Odysseus, the great teller of tales, launched out on
      his story:
'Alcinous, majesty, shining among your island people,
what a fine thing it is to listen to such a bard
as we have here – the man sings like a god.
The crown of life, I'd say. There's nothing better
than when deep joy holds sway throughout the realm
and banqueters up and down the palace sit in ranks,
enthralled to hear the bard, and before them all,
      the tables
heaped with bread and meats, and drawing wine from
      a mixing-bowl
the steward makes his rounds and keeps the winecups
      flowing.
This, to my mind, is the best that life can offer.

                              But now

you're set on probing the bitter pains I've borne,
so I'm to weep and grieve, it seems, still more.
Well then, what shall I go through first,
what shall I save for last?
What pains – the gods have given me my share.
Now let me begin by telling you my name . . .
so you may know it well and I in times to come,
if I can escape the fatal day, will be your host,
your sworn friend, though my home is far from here.

I am Odysseus, son of Laertes, known to the world
for every kind of craft – my fame has reached the skies.
Sunny Ithaca is my home. Atop her stands our seamark,
Mount Neriton's leafy ridges shimmering in the wind.
Around her a ring of islands circle side-by-side,
Dulichion, Same, wooded Zacynthus too, but mine
lies low and away, the farthest out to sea,
rearing into the western dusk
while the others face the east and breaking day.
Mine is a rugged land but good for raising sons –
and I myself, I know no sweeter sight on earth
than a man's own native country.

                                        True enough,
Calypso the lustrous goddess tried to hold me back,
deep in her arching caverns, craving me for a husband.
So did Circe, holding me just as warmly in her halls,
the bewitching queen of Aeaea keen to have me too.
But they never won the heart inside me, never.
So nothing is as sweet as a man's own country,
his own parents, even though he's settled down
in some luxurious house, off in a foreign land
and far from those who bore him.

                                        No more. Come,
let me tell you about the voyage fraught with hardship
Zeus inflicted on me, homeward bound from Troy . . .

    The wind drove me out of Ilium on to Ismarus,
the Cicones' stronghold. There I sacked the city,

killed the men, but as for the wives and plunder,
that rich haul we dragged away from the place –
we shared it round so no one, not on my account,
would go deprived of his fair share of spoils.
Then I urged them to cut and run, set sail,
but would they listen? Not those mutinous fools;
there was too much wine to swill, too many sheep
      to slaughter
down along the beach, and shambling longhorn
      cattle.
And all the while the Cicones sought out other
      Cicones,
called for help from their neighbors living inland:
a larger force, and stronger soldiers too,
skilled hands at fighting men from chariots,
skilled, when a crisis broke, to fight on foot.
Out of the morning mist they came against us –
packed as the leaves and spears that flower forth
      in spring –
and Zeus presented us with disaster, me and my
      comrades
doomed to suffer blow on mortal blow. Lining up,
both armies battled it out against our swift ships,
both raked each other with hurtling bronze lances.
Long as morning rose and the blessed day grew stronger
we stood and fought them off, massed as they were,
      but then,
when the sun wheeled past the hour for unyoking oxen,

3

the Cicones broke our lines and beat us down at last.
Out of each ship, six men-at-arms were killed;
the rest of us rowed away from certain doom.

    From there we sailed on, glad to escape our death
yet sick at heart for the dear companions we had lost.
But I would not let our rolling ships set sail until the
       crews
had raised the triple cry, saluting each poor comrade
cut down by the fierce Cicones on that plain.
Now Zeus who masses the stormclouds hit the fleet
with the North Wind –
            a howling, demonic gale, shrouding over
in thunderheads the earth and sea at once –
                and night swept down
from the sky and the ships went plunging headlong on,
our sails slashed to rags by the hurricane's blast!
We struck them – cringing at death we rowed our ships
to the nearest shoreline, pulled with all our power.
There, for two nights, two days, we lay by, no letup,
eating our hearts out, bent with pain and bone-tired.
When Dawn with her lovely locks brought on the
       third day,
then stepping the masts and hoisting white sails high,
we lounged at the oarlocks, letting wind and helmsmen
keep us true on course . . .
           And now, at long last,
I might have reached my native land unscathed,

but just as I doubled Malea's cape, a tide-rip
and the North Wind drove me way off course
careering past Cythera.

                              Nine whole days
I was borne along by rough, deadly winds
on the fish-infested sea. Then on the tenth
our squadron reached the land of the Lotus-eaters,
people who eat the lotus, mellow fruit and flower.
We disembarked on the coast, drew water there
and crewmen snatched a meal by the swift ships.
Once we'd had our fill of food and drink I sent
a detail ahead, two picked men and a third, a runner,
to scout out who might live there – men like us perhaps,
who live on bread? So off they went and soon enough
they mingled among the natives, Lotus-eaters,

        Lotus-eaters
who had no notion of killing my companions, not at all,
they simply gave them the lotus to taste instead . . .
Any crewmen who ate the lotus, the honey-sweet fruit,
lost all desire to send a message back, much less return,
their only wish to linger there with the Lotus-eaters,
grazing on lotus, all memory of the journey home
dissolved forever. But *I* brought them back, back
to the hollow ships, and streaming tears – I forced them,
hauled them under the rowing benches, lashed them fast
and shouted out commands to my other, steady comrades:
"Quick, no time to lose, embark in the racing ships!" –
so none could eat the lotus, forget the voyage home.

They swung aboard at once, they sat to the oars in ranks
and in rhythm churned the water white with stroke on
      stroke.

    From there we sailed on, our spirits now at a low ebb,
and reached the land of the high and mighty Cyclops,
lawless brutes, who trust so to the everlasting gods
they never plant with their own hands or plow the soil.
Unsown, unplowed, the earth teems with all they need,
wheat, barley and vines, swelled by the rains of Zeus
to yield a big full-bodied wine from clustered grapes.
They have no meeting place for council, no laws either,
no, up on the mountain peaks they live in arching caverns –
each a law to himself, ruling his wives and children,
not a care in the world for any neighbor.
                            Now,
a level island stretches flat across the harbor,
not close inshore to the Cyclops' coast, not too far out,
thick with woods where the wild goats breed by
      hundreds.
No trampling of men to start them from their lairs,
no hunters roughing it out on the woody ridges,
stalking quarry, ever raid their haven.
No flocks browse, no plowlands roll with wheat;
unplowed, unsown forever – empty of humankind –
the island just feeds droves of bleating goats.
For the Cyclops have no ships with crimson prows,

no shipwrights there to build them good trim craft
that could sail them out to foreign ports of call
as most men risk the seas to trade with other men.
Such artisans would have made this island too
a decent place to live in . . . No mean spot,
it could bear you any crop you like in season.
The water-meadows along the low foaming shore
run soft and moist, and your vines would never flag.
The land's clear for plowing. Harvest on harvest,
a man could reap a healthy stand of grain –
the subsoil's dark and rich.
There's a snug deep-water harbor there, what's more,
no need for mooring-gear, no anchor-stones to heave,
no cables to make fast. Just beach your keels, ride out
the days till your shipmates' spirit stirs for open sea
and a fair wind blows. And last, at the harbor's head
there's a spring that rushes fresh from beneath a cave
and black poplars flourish round its mouth.

                                  Well,

here we landed, and surely a god steered us in
through the pitch-black night.
Not that he ever showed himself, with thick fog
swirling around the ships, the moon wrapped in clouds
and not a glimmer stealing through that gloom.
Not one of us glimpsed the island – scanning hard –
or the long combers rolling us slowly toward the coast,
not till our ships had run their keels ashore.

7

Beaching our vessels smoothly, striking sail,
the crews swung out on the low shelving sand
and there we fell asleep, awaiting Dawn's first light.

When young Dawn with her rose-red fingers shone
            once more
we all turned out, intrigued to tour the island.
The local nymphs, the daughters of Zeus himself,
flushed mountain-goats so the crews could make
            their meal.
Quickly we fetched our curved bows and hunting spears
from the ships and, splitting up into three bands,
we started shooting, and soon enough some god
had sent us bags of game to warm our hearts.
A dozen vessels sailed in my command
and to each crew nine goats were shared out
and mine alone took ten. Then all day long
till the sun went down we sat and feasted well
on sides of meat and rounds of heady wine.
The good red stock in our vessels' holds
had not run out, there was still plenty left;
the men had carried off a generous store in jars
when we stormed and sacked the Cicones' holy city.
Now we stared across at the Cyclops' shore, so near
we could even see their smoke, hear their voices,
their bleating sheep and goats . . .
And then when the sun had set and night came on
we lay down and slept at the water's shelving edge.

When young Dawn with her rose-red fingers shone
      once more
I called a muster briskly, commanding all the hands,
"The rest of you stay here, my friends-in-arms.
I'll go across with my own ship and crew
and probe the natives living over there.
What *are* they – violent, savage, lawless?
or friendly to strangers, god-fearing men?"

    With that I boarded ship and told the crew
to embark at once and cast off cables quickly.
They swung aboard, they sat to the oars in ranks
and in rhythm churned the water white with stroke
      on stroke.
But as soon as we reached the coast I mentioned –
      no long trip –
we spied a cavern just at the shore, gaping above
      the surf,
towering, overgrown with laurel. And here big flocks,
sheep and goats, were stalled to spend the nights,
and around its mouth a yard was walled up
with quarried boulders sunk deep in the earth
and enormous pines and oak-trees looming darkly . . .
Here was a giant's lair, in fact, who always pastured
his sheepflocks far afield and never mixed with others.
A grim loner, dead set in his own lawless ways.
Here was a piece of work, by god, a monster
built like no mortal who ever supped on bread,

no, like a shaggy peak, I'd say – a man-mountain
rearing head and shoulders over the world.

Now then,

I told most of my good trusty crew to wait,
to sit tight by the ship and guard her well
while I picked out my dozen finest fighters
and off I went. But I took a skin of wine along,
the ruddy, irresistible wine that Maron gave me once,
Euanthes' son, a priest of Apollo, lord of Ismarus,
because we'd rescued him, his wife and children,
reverent as we were;
he lived, you see, in Apollo's holy grove.
And so in return he gave me splendid gifts,
he handed me seven bars of well-wrought gold,
a mixing-bowl of solid silver, then this wine . . .
He drew it off in generous wine-jars, twelve in all,
all unmixed – and such a bouquet, a drink fit for
        the gods!
No maid or man of his household knew that secret store,
only himself, his loving wife and a single servant.
Whenever they'd drink the deep-red mellow vintage,
twenty cups of water he'd stir in one of wine
and what an aroma wafted from the bowl –
what magic, what a godsend –
no joy in holding back when *that* was poured!
Filling a great goatskin now, I took this wine,
provisions too in a leather sack. A sudden foreboding
told my fighting spirit I'd soon come up against

some giant clad in power like armor-plate –
a savage deaf to justice, blind to law.

Our party quickly made its way to his cave
but we failed to find our host himself inside;
he was off in his pasture, ranging his sleek flocks.
So we explored his den, gazing wide-eyed at it all,
the large flat racks loaded with drying cheeses,
the folds crowded with young lambs and kids,
split into three groups – here the spring-born,
here mid-yearlings, here the fresh sucklings
off to the side – each sort was penned apart.
And all his vessels, pails and hammered buckets
he used for milking, were brimming full with whey.
From the start my comrades pressed me, pleading hard,
"Let's make away with the cheeses, then come back –
hurry, drive the lambs and kids from the pens
to our swift ship, put out to sea at once!"
But I would not give way –
and how much better it would have been –
not till I saw him, saw what gifts he'd give.
But he proved no lovely sight to my companions.

There we built a fire, set our hands on the cheeses,
offered some to the gods and ate the bulk ourselves
and settled down inside, awaiting his return . . .
And back he came from pasture, late in the day,
herding his flocks home, and lugging a huge load

of good dry logs to fuel his fire at supper.
He flung them down in the cave – a jolting crash –
we scuttled in panic into the deepest dark recess.
And next he drove his sleek flocks into the open vault,
all he'd milk at least, but he left the males outside,
rams and billy goats out in the high-walled yard.
Then to close his door he hoisted overhead
a tremendous, massive slab –
no twenty-two wagons, rugged and four-wheeled,
could budge that boulder off the ground, I tell you,
such an immense stone the monster wedged to block
     his cave!
Then down he squatted to milk his sheep and bleating
     goats,
each in order, and put a suckling underneath each dam.
And half of the fresh white milk he curdled quickly,
set it aside in wicker racks to press for cheese,
the other half let stand in pails and buckets,
ready at hand to wash his supper down.
As soon as he'd briskly finished all his chores
he lit his fire and spied us in the blaze and
"Strangers!" he thundered out, "now who are you?
Where did you sail from, over the running sea-lanes?
Out on a trading spree or roving the waves like pirates,
sea-wolves raiding at will, who risk their lives
to plunder other men?"

                The hearts inside us shook,
terrified by his rumbling voice and monstrous hulk.

Nevertheless I found the nerve to answer, firmly,
"Men of Achaea we are and bound now from Troy!
Driven far off course by the warring winds,
over the vast gulf of the sea – battling home
on a strange tack, a route that's off the map,
and so we've come to you . . .
so it must please King Zeus's plotting heart.
We're glad to say we're men of Atrides Agamemnon,
whose fame is the proudest thing on earth these days,
so great a city he sacked, such multitudes he killed!
But since we've chanced on you, we're at your knees
in hopes of a warm welcome, even a guest-gift,
the sort that hosts give strangers. That's the custom.
Respect the gods, my friend. We're suppliants – at your
        mercy!
Zeus of the Strangers guards all guests and suppliants:
strangers are sacred – Zeus will avenge their rights!"

    "Stranger," he grumbled back from his brutal heart,
"you must be a fool, stranger, or come from nowhere,
telling *me* to fear the gods or avoid their wrath!
We Cyclops never blink at Zeus and Zeus's shield
of storm and thunder, or any other blessed god –
we've got more force by far.
I'd never spare you in fear of Zeus's hatred,
you or your comrades here, unless I had the urge.
But tell me, where did you moor your sturdy ship
when you arrived? Up the coast or close in?

I'd just like to know."

So he laid his trap
but he never caught me, no, wise to the world
I shot back in my crafty way, "My ship?
Poseidon god of the earthquake smashed my ship,
he drove it against the rocks at your island's far cape,
he dashed it against a cliff as the winds rode us in.
I and the men you see escaped a sudden death."

Not a word in reply to that, the ruthless brute.
Lurching up, he lunged out with his hands toward
my men
and snatching two at once, rapping them on the ground
he knocked them dead like pups –
their brains gushed out all over, soaked the floor –
and ripping them limb from limb to fix his meal
he bolted them down like a mountain-lion, left no scrap,
devoured entrails, flesh and bones, marrow and all!
We flung our arms to Zeus, we wept and cried aloud,
looking on at his grisly work – paralyzed, appalled.
But once the Cyclops had stuffed his enormous gut
with human flesh, washing it down with raw milk,
he slept in his cave, stretched out along his flocks.
And I with my fighting heart, I thought at first
to steal up to him, draw the sharp sword at my hip
and stab his chest where the midriff packs the liver –
I groped for the fatal spot but a fresh thought held
me back.

There at a stroke we'd finish off ourselves as well –
how could *we* with our bare hands heave back
that slab he set to block his cavern's gaping maw?
So we lay there groaning, waiting Dawn's first light.

When young Dawn with her rose-red fingers shone
    once more
the monster relit his fire and milked his handsome ewes,
each in order, putting a suckling underneath each dam,
and as soon as he'd briskly finished all his chores
he snatched up two more men and fixed his meal.
Well-fed, he drove his fat sheep from the cave,
lightly lifting the huge doorslab up and away,
then slipped it back in place
as a hunter flips the lid of his quiver shut.
Piercing whistles – turning his flocks to the hills
he left me there, the heart inside me brooding on revenge:
how could I pay him back? would Athena give me glory?
Here was the plan that struck my mind as best . . .
the Cyclops' great club: there it lay by the pens,
olivewood, full of sap. He'd lopped it off to brandish
once it dried. Looking it over, we judged it big enough
to be the mast of a pitch-black ship with her twenty oars,
a freighter broad in the beam that plows through
    miles of sea –
so long, so thick it bulked before our eyes. Well,
flanking it now, I chopped off a fathom's length,
rolled it to comrades, told them to plane it down,

and they made the club smooth as I bent and shaved
the tip to a stabbing point. I turned it over
the blazing fire to char it good and hard,
then hid it well, buried deep under the dung
that littered the cavern's floor in thick wet clumps.
And now I ordered my shipmates all to cast lots –
who'd brave it out with me
to hoist our stake and grind it into his eye
when sleep had overcome him? Luck of the draw:
I got the very ones I would have picked myself,
four good men, and I in the lead made five . . .

   Nightfall brought him back, herding his woolly sheep
and he quickly drove the sleek flock into the vaulted
      cavern,
rams and all – none left outside in the walled yard –
his own idea, perhaps, or a god led him on.
Then he hoisted the huge slab to block the door
and squatted to milk his sheep and bleating goats,
each in order, putting a suckling underneath each dam,
and as soon as he'd briskly finished all his chores
he snatched up two more men and fixed his meal.
But this time I lifted a carved wooden bowl,
brimful of my ruddy wine,
and went right up to the Cyclops, enticing,
"Here, Cyclops, try this wine – to top off
the banquet of human flesh you've bolted down!
Judge for yourself what stock our ship had stored.

I brought it here to make you a fine libation,
hoping you would pity me, Cyclops, send me home,
but your rages are insufferable. You barbarian –
how can any man on earth come visit you after *this*?
What you've done outrages all that's right!"

At that he seized the bowl and tossed it off
and the heady wine pleased him immensely – "More" –
he demanded a second bowl – "a hearty helping!
And tell me your name now, quickly,
so I can hand my guest a gift to warm *his* heart.
Our soil yields the Cyclops powerful, full-bodied wine
and the rains from Zeus build its strength. But this,
this is nectar, ambrosia – this flows from heaven!"

So he declared. I poured him another fiery bowl –
three bowls I brimmed and three he drank to the last
                    drop,
the fool, and then, when the wine was swirling round
                    his brain,
I approached my host with a cordial, winning word:
"So, you ask me the name I'm known by, Cyclops?
I will tell you. But you must give me a guest-gift
as you've promised. Nobody – that's my name. Nobody –
so my mother and father call me, all my friends."

But he boomed back at me from his ruthless heart,
"*Nobody?* I'll eat Nobody last of all his friends –

I'll eat the others first! That's my gift to *you*!"

                                                     With that
he toppled over, sprawled full-length, flat on his back
and lay there, his massive neck slumping to one side,
and sleep that conquers all overwhelmed him now
as wine came spurting, flooding up from his gullet
with chunks of human flesh – he vomited, blind drunk.
Now, at last, I thrust our stake in a bed of embers
to get it red-hot and rallied all my comrades:
"Courage – no panic, no one hang back now!"
And green as it was, just as the olive stake
was about to catch fire – the glow terrific, yes –
I dragged it from the flames, my men clustering round
as some god breathed enormous courage through us all.
Hoisting high that olive stake with its stabbing point,
straight into the monster's eye they rammed it hard –
I drove my weight on it from above and bored it home
as a shipwright bores his beam with a shipwright's drill
that men below, whipping the strap back and forth,
     whirl
and the drill keeps twisting faster, never stopping –
So we seized our stake with its fiery tip
and bored it round and round in the giant's eye
till blood came boiling up around that smoking shaft
and the hot blast singed his brow and eyelids round
     the core
and the broiling eyeball burst –
                              its crackling roots blazed

and hissed –

        as a blacksmith plunges a glowing ax or adze
in an ice-cold bath and the metal screeches steam
and its temper hardens – that's the iron's strength –
so the eye of the Cyclops sizzled round that stake!
He loosed a hideous roar, the rock walls echoed round
and we scuttled back in terror. The monster wrenched
        the spike
from his eye and out it came with a red geyser of blood –
he flung it aside with frantic hands, and mad with pain
he bellowed out for help from his neighbor Cyclops
living round about in caves on windswept crags.
Hearing his cries, they lumbered up from every side
and hulking round his cavern, asked what ailed him;
"What, Polyphemus, what in the world's the trouble?
Roaring out in the godsent night to rob us of our
        sleep.
Surely no one's rustling your flocks against your will –
surely no one's trying to kill you now by fraud or
        force!"

"*Nobody*, friends" – Polyphemus bellowed back from
        his cave –
"Nobody's killing me now by fraud and not by force!"

"If you're alone," his friends boomed back at once,
"and nobody's trying to overpower you now – look,
it must be a plague sent here by mighty Zeus

19

and there's no escape from *that*.
You'd better pray to your father, Lord Poseidon.

They lumbered off, but laughter filled my heart
to think how nobody's name – my great cunning stroke –
had duped them one and all. But the Cyclops there,
still groaning, racked with agony, groped around
for the huge slab, and heaving it from the doorway,
down he sat in the cave's mouth, his arms spread wide,
hoping to catch a comrade stealing out with sheep –
such a blithering fool he took me for!
But I was already plotting . . .
what was the best way out? how could I find
escape from death for my crew, myself as well?
My wits kept weaving, weaving cunning schemes –
life at stake, monstrous death staring us in the face –
till this plan struck my mind as best. That flock,
those well-fed rams with their splendid thick fleece,
sturdy, handsome beasts sporting their dark weight
        of wool:
I lashed them abreast, quietly, twisting the willow-twigs
the Cyclops slept on – giant, lawless brute – I took them
three by three; each ram in the middle bore a man
while the two rams either side would shield him well.
So three beasts to bear each man, but as for myself?
There was one bellwether ram, the prize of all the flock,
and clutching him by his back, tucked up under
His shaggy belly, there I hung, face upward,

both hands locked in his marvelous deep fleece,
clinging for dear life, my spirit steeled, enduring . . .
So we held on, desperate, waiting Dawn's first light.

                                              As soon
as young Dawn with her rose-red fingers shone
        once more
the rams went rumbling out of the cave toward pasture,
the ewes kept bleating round the pens, unmilked.
their udders about to burst. Their master now,
heaving in torment, felt the back of each animal
halting before him here, but the idiot never sensed
my men were trussed up under their thick fleecy ribs.
And last of them all came my great ram now, striding out,
weighed down with his dense wool and my deep plots.
Stroking him gently, powerful Polyphemus murmured.
"Dear old ram, why last of the flock to quit the cave?
In the good old days you'd never lag behind the rest –
you with your long marching strides, first by far
of the flock to graze the fresh young grasses,
first by far to reach the rippling streams,
first to turn back home, keen for your fold
when night comes on – but now you're last of all.
And why? Sick at heart for your master's eye
that coward gouged out with his wicked crew? –
only after he'd stunned my wits with wine –
that, that Nobody . . .
who's not escaped his death, I swear, not yet.

Oh if only you thought like *me*, had words like *me*
to tell me where that scoundrel is cringing from my rage!
I'd smash him against the ground, I'd spill his brains –
flooding across my cave – and that would ease my heart
of the pains that good-for-nothing Nobody made me
       suffer!"

    And with that threat he let my ram go free outside.
But soon as we'd got one foot past cave and courtyard,
first I loosed myself from the ram, then loosed my men,
then quickly, glancing back again and again we drove
our flock, good plump beasts with their long shanks,
straight to the ship, and a welcome sight we were
to loyal comrades – we who'd escaped our deaths –
but for all the rest they broke down and wailed.
I cut it short, I stopped each shipmate's cries,
my head tossing, brows frowning, silent signals
to hurry, tumble our fleecy herd on board,
launch out on the open sea!
They swung aboard, they sat to the oars in ranks
and in rhythm churned the water white with stroke on
       stroke.
But once offshore as far as a man's shout can carry,
I called back to the Cyclops, stinging taunts:
"So, Cyclops, no weak coward it was whose crew
you bent to devour there in your vaulted cave –
you with your brute force! Your filthy crimes
came down on your own head, you shameless cannibal,

daring to eat your guests in your own house –
so Zeus and the other gods have paid you back!"

That made the rage of the monster boil over.
Ripping off the peak of a towering crag, he heaved it
so hard the boulder landed just in front of our dark prow
and a huge swell reared up as the rock went plunging under –
a tidal wave from the open sea. The sudden backwash
drove us landward again, forcing us close inshore
but grabbing a long pole, I thrust us off and away,
tossing my head for dear life, signaling crews
to put their backs in the oars, escape grim death.
They threw themselves in the labor, rowed on fast
but once we'd plowed the breakers twice as far,
again I began to taunt the Cyclops – men around me
trying to check me, calm me, left and right:
"So headstrong – why? Why rile the beast again?"

"That rock he flung in the sea just now, hurling our ship
to shore once more – we thought we'd die on the spot!"

"If he'd caught a sound from one of us, just a moan,
he would have crushed our heads and ship timbers
with one heave of another flashing, jagged rock!"

"Good god, the brute can throw!"

So they begged
but they could not bring my fighting spirit round.

23

I called back with another burst of anger, "Cyclops –
if any man on the face of the earth should ask you
who blinded you, shamed you so – say Odysseus,
raider of cities, *he* gouged out your eye,
Laertes' son who makes his home in Ithaca!"

So I vaunted and he groaned back in answer,
"Oh no, no – that prophecy years ago . . .
it all comes home to me with a vengeance now!
We once had a prophet here, a great tall man,
Telemus, Eurymus' son, a master at reading signs,
who grew old in his trade among his fellow-Cyclops.
All this, he warned me, would come to pass someday –
that I'd be blinded here at the hands of one Odysseus.
But I always looked for a handsome giant man to cross
        my path,
some fighter clad in power like armor-plate, but now,
look what a dwarf, a spineless good-for-nothing,
stuns me with wine, then gouges out my eye!
Come here, Odysseus, let me give you a guest-gift
and urge Poseidon the earthquake god to speed
        you home.
I am his son and he claims to be my father, true,
and he himself will heal me if he pleases –
no other blessed god, no man can do the work!"

                                        "Heal you!" –
here was my parting shot – "Would to god I could
        strip you

of life and breath and ship you down to the House
    of Death
as surely as no one will ever heal your eye,
not even your earthquake god himself!"

But at that he bellowed out to lord Poseidon,
thrusting his arms to the starry skies, and prayed, "Hear me –
Poseidon, god of the sea-blue mane who rocks the earth!
If I really am your son and you claim to be my father –
come, grant that Odysseus, raider of cities,
Laertes' son who makes his home in Ithaca,
never reaches home. Or if he's fated to see
his people once again and reach his well-built house
and his own native country, let him come home late
and come a broken man – all shipmates lost,
alone in a stranger's ship –
and let him find a world of pain at home!"

                           So he prayed
and the god of the sea-blue mane, Poseidon, heard his
    prayer.
The monster suddenly hoisted a boulder – far larger –
wheeled and heaved it, putting his weight behind it,
massive strength, and the boulder crashed close,
landing just in the wake of our dark stern,
just failing to graze the rudder's bladed edge.
A huge swell reared up as the rock went plunging under,
yes, and the tidal breaker drove us out to our island's
far shore where all my well-decked ships lay moored,

clustered, waiting, and huddled round them, crewmen
sat in anguish, waiting, chafing for our return.
We beached our vessel hard ashore on the sand,
we swung out in the frothing surf ourselves,
and herding Cyclops' sheep from our deep holds
we shared them round so no one, not on my account,
would go deprived of his fair share of spoils.
But the splendid ram – as we meted out the flocks
my friends-in-arms made him my prize of honor,
mine alone, and I slaughtered him on the beach
and burnt his thighs to Cronus' mighty son,
Zeus of the thundercloud who rules the world.
But my sacrifices failed to move the god:
Zeus was still obsessed with plans to destroy
my entire oarswept fleet and loyal crew of comrades.
Now all day long till the sun went down we sat
and feasted on sides of meat and heady wine.
Then when the sun had set and night came on
we lay down and slept at the water's shelving edge.
When young Dawn with her rose-red fingers shone
        once more
I roused the men straightway, ordering all crews
to man the ships and cast off cables quickly.
They swung aboard at once, they sat to the oars in ranks
and in rhythm churned the water white with stroke
        on stroke.
And from there we sailed on, glad to escape our death
yet sick at heart for the comrades we had lost."

The Bewitching Queen of Aeaea

'We reached the Aeolian island next, the home of Aeolus,
Hippotas' son, beloved by the gods who never die –
a great floating island it was, and round it all
huge ramparts rise of indestructible bronze
and sheer rock cliffs shoot up from sea to sky.
The king had sired twelve children within his halls,
six daughters and six sons in the lusty prime of youth,
so he gave his daughters as wives to his six sons.
Seated beside their dear father and doting mother,
with delicacies aplenty spread before them,
they feast on forever . . . All day long
the halls breathe the savor of roasted meats
and echo round to the low moan of blowing pipes,
and all night long, each one by his faithful mate,
they sleep under soft-piled rugs on corded bedsteads.
To this city of theirs we came, their splendid palace,
and Aeolus hosted me one entire month, he pressed me
        for news
of Troy and the Argive ships and how we sailed for
        home,
and I told him the whole long story, first to last.
And then, when I begged him to send me on my way,
he denied me nothing, he went about my passage.
He gave me a sack, the skin of a full-grown ox,
binding inside the winds that howl from every quarter,

27

for Zeus had made that king the master of all the winds,
with power to calm them down or rouse them as he
     pleased.
Aeolus stowed the sack inside my holds, lashed so fast
with a burnished silver cord
not even a slight puff could slip past that knot.
Yet he set the West Wind free to blow us on our way
and waft our squadron home. But his plan was bound
     to fail,
yes, our own reckless folly swept us on to ruin . . .

    Nine whole days we sailed, nine nights, nonstop.
On the tenth our own land hove into sight at last –
we were so close we could see men tending fires.
But now an enticing sleep came on me, bone-weary
from working the vessel's sheet myself, no letup,
never trusting the ropes to any other mate,
the faster to journey back to native land.
But the crews began to mutter among themselves,
sure I was hauling troves of gold and silver home,
the gifts of open-hearted Aeolus, Hippotas' son.
"The old story!" One man glanced at another,
     grumbling.
"Look at our captain's luck – so loved by the world,
so prized at every landfall, every port of call."

    "Heaps of lovely plunder he hauls home from Troy,
while we who went through slogging just as hard,

we go home empty-handed."
                              "Now this Aeolus loads him
down with treasure. Favoritism, friend to friend!"

"Hurry, let's see what loot is in that sack,
how much gold and silver. Break it open – now!"

A fatal plan, but it won my shipmates over.
They loosed the sack and all the winds burst out
and a sudden squall struck and swept us back to sea,
wailing, in tears, far from our own native land.
And I woke up with a start, my spirit churning –
should I leap over the side and drown at once or
grit my teeth and bear it, stay among the living?
I bore it all, held firm, hiding my face,
clinging tight to the decks
while heavy squalls blasted our squadron back
again to Aeolus' island, shipmates groaning hard.

We disembarked on the coast, drew water there
and crewmen snatched a meal by the swift ships.
Once we'd had our fill of food and drink
I took a shipmate along with me, a herald too,
and approached King Aeolus' famous halls and here
we found him feasting beside his wife and many
        children.
Reaching the doorposts at the threshold, down we sat
but our hosts, amazed to see us, only shouted questions:

"Back again, Odysseus – why? Some blustering god
        attacked you?
Surely we launched you well, we sped you on your way
to your own land and house, or any place you pleased."

So they taunted, and I replied in deep despair,
"A mutinous crew undid me – that and a cruel sleep.
Set it to rights, my friends. You have the power!"

So I pleaded – gentle, humble appeals –
but our hosts turned silent, hushed . . .
and the father broke forth with an ultimatum:
"Away from my island – fast – most cursed man alive!
It's a crime to host a man or speed him on his way
when the blessed deathless gods despise him so.
Crawling back like this –
it proves the immortals hate you! Out – get out!"

Groan as I did, his curses drove me from his halls
and from there we pulled away with heavy hearts,
with the crews' spirit broken under the oars' labor,
thanks to our own folly . . . no favoring wind in sight.

Six whole days we rowed, six nights, nonstop.
On the seventh day we raised the Laestrygonian land,
Telepylus heights where the craggy fort of Lamus rises.
Where shepherd calls to shepherd as one drives in his
        flocks

and the other drives his out and he calls back in answer,
where a man who never sleeps could rake in double wages,
one for herding cattle, one for pasturing fleecy sheep,
the nightfall and the sunrise march so close together.
We entered a fine harbor there, all walled around
by a great unbroken sweep of sky-scraping cliff
and two steep headlands, fronting each other, close
around the mouth so the passage in is cramped.
Here the rest of my rolling squadron steered,
right into the gaping cove and moored tightly,
prow by prow. Never a swell there, big or small;
a milk-white calm spreads all around the place.
But I alone anchored my black ship outside,
well clear of the harbor's jaws
I tied her fast to a cliffside with a cable.
I scaled its rock face to a lookout on its crest
but glimpsed no trace of the work of man or beast
        from there;
all I spied was a plume of smoke, drifting off the land.
So I sent some crew ahead to learn who lived there –
men like us perhaps, who live on bread?
Two good mates I chose and a third to run the news.
They disembarked and set out on a beaten trail
the wagons used for hauling timber down to town
from the mountain heights above . . .
and before the walls they met a girl, drawing water,
Antiphates' strapping daughter – king of the
        Laestrygonians.

She'd come down to a clear running spring, Artacia,
where the local people came to fill their pails.
My shipmates clustered round her, asking questions:
who was king of the realm? who ruled the natives here?
She waved at once to her father's high-roofed halls.
They entered the sumptuous palace, found his wife inside –
a woman huge as a mountain crag who filled them all
          with horror.
Straightaway she summoned royal Antiphates from
          assembly,
her husband, who prepared my crew a barbarous
          welcome.
Snatching one of my men, he tore him up for dinner –
the other two sprang free and reached the ships.
But the king let loose a howling through the town
that brought tremendous Laestrygonians swarming up
from every side – hundreds, not like men, like Giants!
Down from the cliffs they flung great rocks a man could
          hardly hoist
and a ghastly shattering din rose up from all the ships –
men in their death-cries, hulls smashed to splinters –
They speared the crews like fish
and whisked them home to make their grisly meal.
But while they killed them off in the harbor depths
I pulled the sword from beside my hip and hacked away
at the ropes that moored my blue-prowed ship of war
and shouted rapid orders at my shipmates:
"Put your backs in the oars – now row or die!"

In terror of death they ripped the swells – all as one –
and what a joy as we darted out toward open sea,
clear of those beetling cliffs . . . my ship alone.
But the rest went down en masse. Our squadron sank.

From there we sailed on, glad to escape our death
yet sick at heart for the dear companions we had lost.
We reached the Aeaean island next, the home of Circe
the nymph with lovely braids, an awesome power too
who can speak with human voice,
the true sister of murderous-minded Aeetes.
Both were bred by the Sun who lights our lives;
their mother was Perse, a child the Ocean bore.
We brought our ship to port without a sound
as a god eased her into a harbor safe and snug,
and for two days and two nights we lay by there,
eating our hearts out, bent with pain and bone-tired.
When Dawn with her lovely locks brought on the
          third day,
at last I took my spear and my sharp sword again,
rushed up from the ship to find a lookout point,
hoping to glimpse some sign of human labor,
catch some human voices . . .
I scaled a commanding crag and, scanning hard,
I could just make out some smoke from Circe's halls,
drifting up from the broad terrain through brush
          and woods.
Mulling it over, I thought I'd scout the ground –

that fire aglow in the smoke, I saw it, true,
but soon enough this seemed the better plan:
I'd go back to shore and the swift ship first,
feed the men, then send *them* out for scouting.
I was well on my way down, nearing our ship
when a god took pity on me, wandering all alone;
he sent me a big stag with high branching antlers,
right across my path – the sun's heat forced him down
from his forest range to drink at a river's banks –
just bounding out of the timber when I hit him
square in the backbone, halfway down the spine
and my bronze spear went punching clean through –
he dropped in the dust, groaning, gasping out his breath.
Treading on him, I wrenched my bronze spear from
      the wound,
left it there on the ground, and snapping off some twigs
and creepers, twisted a rope about a fathom long,
I braided it tight, hand over hand, then lashed
the four hocks of that magnificent beast.
Loaded round my neck I lugged him toward the ship,
trudging, propped on my spear – no way to sling him
over a shoulder, steadying him with one free arm –
the kill was so immense!
I flung him down by the hull and roused the men,
going up to them all with a word to lift their spirits:
"Listen to me, my comrades, brothers in hardship –
we won't go down to the House of Death, not yet,

not till our day arrives. Up with you, look,
there's still some meat and drink in our good ship.
Put our minds on food – why die of hunger here?"

My hardy urging brought them round at once.
Heads came up from cloaks and there by the
        barren sea
they gazed at the stag, their eyes wide – my noble
        trophy.
But once they'd looked their fill and warmed their
        hearts,
they washed their hands and prepared a splendid
        meal.
Now all day long till the sun went down we sat
and feasted on sides of meat and seasoned wine.
Then when the sun had set and night came on
we lay down and slept at the water's shelving edge.
When young Dawn with her rose-red fingers shone
        once more
I called a muster quickly, informing all the crew,
"Listen to me, my comrades, brothers in hardship,
we can't tell east from west, the dawn from the dusk,
nor where the sun that lights our lives goes under earth
nor where it rises. We must think of a plan at once,
some cunning stroke. I doubt there's one still left.
I scaled a commanding crag and from that height
surveyed an entire island

ringed like a crown by endless wastes of sea.
But the land itself lies low, and I did see smoke
drifting up from its heart through thick brush and
      woods."

My message broke their spirit as they recalled
the gruesome work of the Laestrygonian king Antiphates
and the hearty cannibal Cyclops thirsting for our blood.
They burst into cries, wailing, streaming live tears
that gained us nothing – what good can come of grief?

And so, numbering off my band of men-at-arms
into two platoons, I assigned them each a leader:
I took one and lord Eurylochus the other.
We quickly shook lots in a bronze helmet –
the lot of brave Eurylochus leapt out first.
So he moved off with his two and twenty comrades,
weeping, leaving us behind in tears as well . . .
Deep in the wooded glens they came on Circe's palace
built of dressed stone on a cleared rise of land.
Mountain wolves and lions were roaming round the grounds –
she'd bewitched them herself, she gave them magic drugs.
But they wouldn't attack my men; they just came pawing
up around them, fawning, swishing their long tails –
eager as hounds that fawn around their master,
coming home from a feast,
who always brings back scraps to calm them down.
So they came nuzzling round my men – lions, wolves

with big powerful claws – and the men cringed in fear
at the sight of those strange, ferocious beasts . . . But still
they paused at her doors, the nymph with lovely braids,
Circe – and deep inside they heard her singing, lifting
her spellbinding voice as she glided back and forth
at her great immortal loom, her enchanting web
a shimmering glory only goddesses can weave.
Polites, captain of armies, took command,
the closest, most devoted man I had: "Friends,
there's someone inside, plying a great loom,
and how she sings – enthralling!
The whole house is echoing to her song.
Goddess or woman – let's call out to her now!"

So he urged and the men called out and hailed her.
She opened her gleaming doors at once and stepped
        forth,
inviting them all in, and in they went, all innocence.
Only Eurylochus stayed behind – he sensed a trap . . .
She ushered them in to sit on high-backed chairs,
then she mixed them a potion – cheese, barley
and pale honey mulled in Pramnian wine –
but into the brew she stirred her wicked drugs
to wipe from their memories any thought of home.
Once they'd drained the bowls she filled, suddenly
she struck with her wand, drove them into her pigsties,
all of them bristling into swine – with grunts,
snouts – even their bodies, yes, and only

the men's minds stayed steadfast as before.
So off they went to their pens, sobbing, squealing
as Circe flung them acorns, cornel nuts and mast,
common fodder for hogs that root and roll in mud.

Back Eurylochus ran to our swift black ship
to tell the disaster our poor friends had faced.
But try as he might, he couldn't get a word out.
Numbing sorrow had stunned the man to silence –
tears welled in his eyes, his heart possessed by grief.
We assailed him with questions – all at our wits' end –
till at last he could recount the fate our friends had met:
"Off we went through the brush, captain, as you
        commanded.
Deep in the wooded glens we came on Circe's palace
built of dressed stone on a cleared rise of land.
Someone inside was plying a great loom,
and how she sang – in a high clear voice!
Goddess or woman – we called out and hailed her . . .
She opened her gleaming doors at once and stepped
        forth,
inviting us all in, and in we went, all innocence.
But *I* stayed behind – I sensed a trap. Suddenly
all vanished – blotted out – not one face showed again,
though I sat there keeping watch a good long time."

At that report I slung the hefty bronze blade
of my silver-studded sword around my shoulder,

slung my bow on too and told our comrade,
"Lead me back by the same way that you came."
But he flung both arms around my knees and pleaded,
begging me with his tears and winging words:
"Don't force me back there, captain, king –
leave me here on the spot.
You will never return yourself, I swear,
you'll never bring back a single man alive.
Quick, cut and run with the rest of us here –
we can still escape the fatal day!"

But I shot back, "Eurylochus, stay right here,
eating, drinking, safe by the black ship.
I must be off. Necessity drives me on."

Leaving the ship and shore, I headed inland,
clambering up through hushed, entrancing glades until,
as I was nearing the halls of Circe skilled in spells,
approaching her palace – Hermes god of the
      golden wand
crossed my path, and he looked for all the world
like a young man sporting his first beard,
just in the prime and warm pride of youth,
and grasped me by the hand and asked me kindly,
"Where are you going now, my unlucky friend –
trekking over the hills alone in unfamiliar country?
And your men are all in there, in Circe's palace,
cooped like swine, hock by jowl in the sties.

39

Have you come to set them free?
Well, I warn you, you won't get home yourself,
you'll stay right there, trapped with all the rest.
But wait, I can save you, free you from that great danger.
Look, here is a potent drug. Take it to Circe's halls –
its power alone will shield you from the fatal day.
Let me tell you of all the witch's subtle craft . . .
She'll mix you a potion, lace the brew with drugs
but she'll be powerless to bewitch you, even so –
this magic herb I give will fight her spells.
Now here's your plan of action, step by step.
The moment Circe strikes with her long thin wand,
you draw your sharp sword sheathed at your hip
and rush her fast as if to run her through!
She'll cower in fear and coax you to her bed –
but don't refuse the goddess' bed, not then, not if
she's to release your friends and treat you well yourself.
But have her swear the binding oath of the blessed gods
she'll never plot some new intrigue to harm you,
once you lie there naked –
never unman you, strip away your courage!"

                                   With that
the giant-killer handed over the magic herb,
pulling it from the earth,
and Hermes showed me all its name and nature.
Its root is black and its flower white as milk
and the gods call it moly. Dangerous for a mortal man
to pluck from the soil but not for deathless gods.

All lies within their power.
Now Hermes went his way
to the steep heights of Olympus, over the island's woods
while I, just approaching the halls of Circe,
my heart a heaving storm at every step,
paused at her doors, the nymph with lovely braids –
I stood and shouted to her there. She heard my voice,
she opened her gleaming doors at once and stepped
      forth,
inviting me in, and in I went, all anguish now . . .
She led me in to sit on a silver-studded chair,
ornately carved, with a stool to rest my feet.
In a golden bowl she mixed a potion for me to drink,
stirring her poison in, her heart aswirl with evil.
And then she passed it on, I drank it down
but it never worked its spell –
she struck with her wand and "Now," she cried,
"off to your sty, you swine, and wallow with your friends!"
But I, I drew my sharp sword sheathed at my hip
and rushed her fast as if to run her through –
She screamed, slid under my blade, hugged my knees
with a flood of warm tears and a burst of winging words:
"Who are you? where are you from? your city?
      your parents?
I'm wonderstruck – you drank my drugs, you're
      not bewitched!
Never has any other man withstood my potion, never,
once it's past his lips and he has drunk it down.

41

You have a mind in *you* no magic can enchant!
You must be Odysseus, man of twists and turns –
Hermes the giant-killer, god of the golden wand,
he always said you'd come,
homeward bound from Troy in your swift black ship.
Come, sheathe your sword, let's go to bed together,
mount my bed and mix in the magic work of love –
we'll breed deep trust between us."

                                             So she enticed
but I fought back, still wary. "Circe, Circe,
how dare you tell me to treat you with any warmth?
You who turned my men to swine in your own house
       and now
you hold me here as well – teeming with treachery
you lure me to your room to mount your bed,
so once I lie there naked
you'll unman me, strip away my courage!
Mount your bed? Not for all the world. Not
until you consent to swear, goddess, a binding oath
you'll never plot some new intrigue to harm me!"

                                           Straightaway
she began to swear the oath that I required – never,
she'd never do me harm – and when she'd finished,
then, at last, I mounted Circe's gorgeous bed . . .

   At the same time her handmaids bustled through
       the halls,
four in all who perform the goddess' household tasks:

nymphs, daughters born of the springs and groves
and the sacred rivers running down to open sea.
One draped the chairs with fine crimson covers
over the seats she'd spread with linen cloths below.
A second drew up silver tables before the chairs
and laid out golden trays to hold the bread.
A third mulled heady, heart-warming wine
in a silver bowl and set out golden cups.
A fourth brought water and lit a blazing fire
beneath a massive cauldron. The water heated soon,
and once it reached the boil in the glowing bronze
she eased me into a tub and bathed me from
     the cauldron,
mixing the hot and cold to suit my taste, showering
head and shoulders down until she'd washed away
the spirit-numbing exhaustion from my body.
The bathing finished, rubbing me sleek with oil,
throwing warm fleece and a shirt around my shoulders,
she led me in to sit on a silver-studded chair,
ornately carved, with a stool to rest my feet.
A maid brought water soon in a graceful golden pitcher
and over a silver basin tipped it out
so I might rinse my hands,
then pulled a gleaming table to my side.
A staid housekeeper brought on bread to serve me,
appetizers aplenty too, lavish with her bounty.
She pressed me to eat. I had no taste for food.
I just sat there, mind wandering, far away . . .

lost in grim forebodings.

As soon as Circe saw me,
huddled, not touching my food, immersed in sorrow,
she sidled near with a coaxing, winged word:
"Odysseus, why just sit there, struck dumb,
eating your heart out, not touching food or drink?
Suspect me of still more treachery? Nothing to fear.
Haven't I just sworn my solemn, binding oath?"

So she asked, but I protested, "Circe –
how could any man in his right mind endure
the taste of food and drink before he'd freed
his comrades-in-arms and looked them in the eyes?
If you, you really want me to eat and drink,
set them free, all my beloved comrades –
let me feast my eyes."

So I demanded.
Circe strode on through the halls and out,
her wand held high in hand and, flinging open the
        pens,
drove forth my men, who looked like full-grown swine.
Facing her, there they stood as she went along
        the ranks,
anointing them one by one with some new magic oil –
and look, the bristles grown by the first wicked drug
that Circe gave them slipped away from their limbs
and they turned men again: younger than ever,
taller by far, more handsome to the eye, and yes,

they knew me at once and each man grasped my hands
and a painful longing for tears overcame us all,
a terrible sobbing echoed through the house . . .
The goddess herself was moved and, standing by me,
warmly urged me on – a lustrous goddess now:
"Royal son of Laertes, Odysseus, tried and true,
go at once to your ship at the water's edge,
haul her straight up on the shore first
and stow your cargo and running gear in caves,
then back you come and bring your trusty crew."

    Her urging won my stubborn spirit over.
Down I went to the swift ship at the water's edge,
and there on the decks I found my loyal crew
consumed with grief and weeping live warm tears.
But now, as calves in stalls when cows come home,
droves of them herded back from field to farmyard
once they've grazed their fill – as all their young calves
come frisking out to meet them, bucking out of
       their pens,
lowing nonstop, jostling, rushing round their mothers –
so my shipmates there at the sight of my return
came pressing round me now, streaming tears,
so deeply moved in their hearts they felt as if
they'd made it back to their own land, their city,
Ithaca's rocky soil where they were bred and reared.
And through their tears their words went winging
       home:

"You're back again, my king! How thrilled we are –
as if we'd reached our country, Ithaca, at last!
But come, tell us about the fate our comrades met."

Still I replied with a timely word of comfort:
"Let's haul our ship straight up on the shore first
and stow our cargo and running gear in caves.
Then hurry, all of you, come along with me
to see our friends in the magic halls of Circe,
eating and drinking – the feast flows on forever."

So I said and they jumped to do my bidding.
Only Eurylochus tried to hold my shipmates back,
his mutinous outburst aimed at one and all:
"Poor fools, where are we running now?
Why are we tempting fate? –
why stumble blindly down to Circe's halls?
She'll turn us all into pigs or wolves or lions
made to guard that palace of hers – by force, I tell you –
just as the Cyclops trapped our comrades in his lair
with hotheaded Odysseus right beside them all –
thanks to this man's rashness they died too!'

So he declared and I had half a mind
to draw the sharp sword from beside my hip
and slice his head off, tumbling down in the dust,
close kin that he was. But comrades checked me,
each man trying to calm me, left and right:

"Captain, we'll leave him here if you command,
just where he is, to sit and guard the ship.
Lead us on to the magic halls of Circe."

                      With that,
up from the ship and shore they headed inland.
Nor did Eurylochus malinger by the hull;
he straggled behind the rest,
dreading the sharp blast of my rebuke.

                      All the while
Circe had bathed my other comrades in her palace,
caring and kindly, rubbed them sleek with oil
and decked them out in fleecy cloaks and shirts.
We found them all together, feasting in her halls.
Once we had recognized each other, gazing face-to-face,
we all broke down and wept – and the house
        resounded now
and Circe the lustrous one came toward me, pleading,
"Royal son of Laertes, Odysseus, man of action,
no more tears now, calm these tides of sorrow.
Well I know what pains you bore on the swarming sea,
what punishment you endured from hostile men
        on land.
But come now, eat your food and drink your wine
till the same courage fills your chests, now as then,
when you first set sail from native land, from rocky
        Ithaca!
Now you are burnt-out husks, your spirits haggard, sere,
always brooding over your wanderings long and hard,

47

your hearts never lifting with any joy –
you've suffered far too much."
                                    So she enticed
and won our battle-hardened spirits over.
And there we sat at ease,
day in, day out, till a year had run its course,
feasting on sides of meat and drafts of heady wine . . .
But then, when the year was gone and the seasons
        wheeled by
and the months waned and the long days came round
        again,
my loyal comrades took me aside and prodded,
"Captain, this is madness!
High time you thought of your own home at last,
if it really is your fate to make it back alive
and reach your well-built house and native land."

    Their urging brought my stubborn spirit round.
So all that day till the sun went down we sat
and feasted on sides of meat and heady wine.
Then when the sun had set and night came on
the men lay down to sleep in the shadowed halls
but I went up to that luxurious bed of Circe's,
hugged her by the knees
and the goddess heard my winging supplication:
"Circe, now make good a promise you gave me once –
it's time to help me home. My heart longs to be home,
my comrades' hearts as well. They wear me down,

pleading with me whenever you're away."

So I pressed

and the lustrous goddess answered me in turn:
"Royal son of Laertes, Odysseus, old campaigner,
stay on no more in my house against your will.
But first another journey calls. You must travel down
to the House of Death and the awesome one,

Persephone,

there to consult the ghost of Tiresias, seer of Thebes,
the great blind prophet whose mind remains unshaken.
Even in death – Persephone has given him wisdom,
everlasting vision to him and him alone . . .
the rest of the dead are empty, flitting shades."

So she said and crushed the heart inside me.
I knelt in her bed and wept. I'd no desire
to go on living and see the rising light of day.
But once I'd had my fill of tears and writhing there,
at last I found the words to venture, "Circe, Circe,
who can pilot us on that journey? Who has ever
reached the House of Death in a black ship?"

The lustrous goddess answered, never pausing,
"Royal son of Laertes, Odysseus, born for exploits,
let no lack of a pilot at the helm concern you, no,
just step your mast and spread your white sail wide –
sit back and the North Wind will speed you on your way.
But once your vessel has cut across the Ocean River

you will raise a desolate coast and Persephone's Grove,
her tall black poplars, willows whose fruit dies young.
Beach your vessel hard by the Ocean's churning shore
and make your own way down to the moldering House
      of Death.
And there into Acheron, the Flood of Grief, two
      rivers flow,
the torrent River of Fire, the wailing River of Tears
that branches off from Styx, the Stream of Hate,
and a stark crag looms
where the two rivers thunder down and meet.
Once there, go forward, hero. Do as I say now.
Dig a trench of about a forearm's depth and length
and around it pour libations out to all the dead –
first with milk and honey, and then with mellow wine,
then water third and last, and sprinkle glistening
      barley
over it all, and vow again and again to all the dead,
to the drifting, listless spirits of their ghosts,
that once you return to Ithaca you will slaughter
a barren heifer in your halls, the best you have,
and load a pyre with treasures – and to Tiresias,
alone, apart, you will offer a sleek black ram,
the pride of all your herds. And once your prayers
have invoked the nations of the dead in their
      dim glory,
slaughter a ram and a black ewe, turning both
      their heads

toward Erebus, but turn your head away, looking
      toward
the Ocean River. Suddenly then the countless shades
of the dead and gone will surge around you there.
But order your men at once to flay the sheep
that lie before you, killed by your ruthless blade,
and burn them both, and then say prayers to the gods,
to the almighty god of death and dread Persephone.
But you – draw your sharp sword from beside
      your hip,
sit down on alert there, and never let the ghosts
of the shambling, shiftless dead come near that blood
till you have questioned Tiresias yourself. Soon, soon
the great seer will appear before you, captain of armies:
he will tell you the way to go, the stages of your voyage,
how you can cross the swarming sea and reach home
      at last."

    And with those words Dawn rose on her golden
      throne
and Circe dressed me quickly in sea-cloak and shirt
while the queen slipped on a loose, glistening robe,
filmy, a joy to the eye, and round her waist
she ran a brocaded golden belt
and over her head a scarf to shield her brow.
And I strode on through the halls to stir my men,
hovering over each with a winning word: "Up now!
No more lazing away in sleep, we must set sail –

Queen Circe has shown the way."

I brought them round,
my hardy friends-in-arms, but not even from there
could I get them safely off without a loss . . .
There was a man, Elpenor, the youngest in our ranks,
none too brave in battle, none too sound in mind.
He'd strayed from his mates in Circe's magic halls
and keen for the cool night air,
sodden with wine he'd bedded down on her roofs.
But roused by the shouts and tread of marching men,
he leapt up with a start at dawn but still so dazed
he forgot to climb back down again by the long
     ladder –
headfirst from the roof he plunged, his neck snapped
from the backbone, his soul flew down to Death.

Once on our way, I gave the men their orders:
"You think we are headed home, our own dear land?
Well, Circe sets us a rather different course . . .
down to the House of Death and the awesome one,
     Persephone,
there to consult the ghost of Tiresias, seer of Thebes."

So I said, and it broke my shipmates' hearts.
They sank down on the ground, moaning, tore their
     hair.
But it gained us nothing – what good can come of
     grief?

Back to the swift ship at the water's edge we went,
our spirits deep in anguish, faces wet with tears.
But Circe got to the dark hull before us,
tethered a ram and black ewe close by –
slipping past unseen. Who can glimpse a god
who wants to be invisible gliding here and there?"